D1266723

Pink As a Piglet

Rosa como un cerdito

written by **Molly Dingles**
illustrated by **Walter Velez**

dingles&company New Jersey

For Lauren & Kelli

©2004 by Judith Mazzeo Zocchi

All rights reserved.
No part of this book may be reproduced in any form
without written permission from the publishers,
except by a reviewer who may quote brief passages
in a review to be printed in a newspaper or magazine.

First printing

PUBLISHED BY dingles&company
P.O. Box 508 • Sea Girt, New Jersey • 08750
WEBSITE: www.dingles.com • E-MAIL: info@dingles.com

LIBRARY BINDING EDITION DISTRIBUTED BY **GUMDROP BOOKS**
P.O. Box 505 • Bethany, Missouri • 64424
(660) 425-7777

Library of Congress Catalog Card No.: 2003115147
ISBN: 1-891997-34-3

Printed in the United States of America

●

ART DIRECTED & DESIGNED BY Barbie Lambert

ENGLISH TEXT EDITED BY Andrea Curley

SPANISH TEXT EDITED BY John Page

EDUCATION CONSULTANT Kathleen P. Miller

Molly Dingles

is the author of *Jinka Jinka Jelly Bean* and *Little Lee Lee's Birthday Bang*. As Judy Zocchi, she has written the *Paulie & Sasha* series. She is a writer and lyricist who holds a bachelor's degree in fine arts/theater from Mount Saint Mary's College and a master's degree in educational theater from New York University. She lives in Manasquan, New Jersey, with her husband, David.

Walter Velez

was born in New York. He attended the High School of Art and Design and later the School of Visual Arts. He has done illustration work for many major book and gaming companies. He is known for the popular series *Thieves World* as well as the *Myth* series for Ace Books. He has also produced trading cards for *Goosebumps* and *Dune*. In addition, Walter has illustrated several *Star Wars* books for Random House. He lives in Queens, New York, with his wife, Kriti, and daughter, Kassandra.

The Community of Color series is more than just a series of books about colors. The series demonstrates how individual people, places, and things combine to form a community. It allows children to view the world in segments and then experience the wonderment and value of the community as a whole.

Pink as a banner

Rosa como una banderola

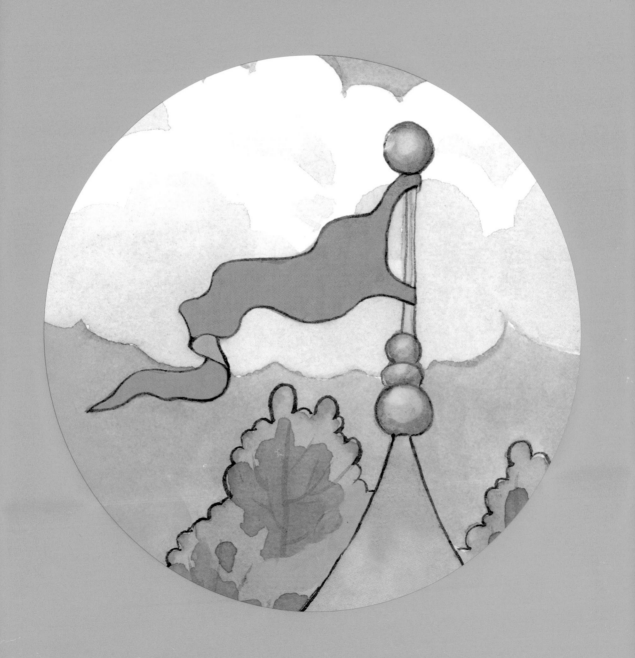

Pink **Ferris wheel**

Rueda Chicago rosa

Pink cotton candy

Algodón dulce **rosa**

Pink feathers to feel

Plumas rosas que sentir

Pink as a piglet

Rosa como un cerdito

Pink bubblegum

Chicle rosa

Pink ballet slippers

Zapatillas de ballet rosas

Pink ring on a thumb

Anillo rosa en un pulgar

Pink as a ribbon

Rosa como un listón

Pink poodle hair

Pelo de caniche rosa

Pink paper tickets

Boletos de papel rosa

**Pink ice cream
to share**

**Helado rosa
para compartir**

The color Pink
is all around.

El color Rosa está
en todas partes.

Where at this carnival can Pink be found?

¿En qué parte de este carnaval se puede encontrar el Rosa?

ABOUT COLOR

Use the Community of Color series to teach your child to identify the most basic colors and to help him or her relate these colors to objects in the real world. ASK:

- What color is this book about?
- Can you name the pink things at this carnival?
- How many pink ice-cream cones can you find?
- How many different shades of pink are in this picture?

ABOUT COMMUNITY

Use the Community of Color series to teach your child how he or she is an important part of the community. Explain to your child what a community is.

- A community is a place where people live, work, and play together.
- Your family is a community.
- Your school is a community.
- Your neighborhood is a community.
- The world is one big community.

Everyone plays an important part in making a community work - moms, dads, boys, girls, police officers, firefighters, teachers, mail carriers, garbage collectors, store clerks, and even animals are all important parts of a community. USE THESE QUESTIONS TO FURTHER THE CONVERSATION:

- How are the people at this carnival interacting with one another?
- How are the people different from one another? How are they the same?
- What do they have in common?
- How is the community you see in this book like your community? How is it different?
- Describe your community.

ABOUT FEELINGS

Colors can describe as well as evoke different emotions. Encourage your child to describe the feelings that the color pink inspires. ASK:

- How does the color pink make you feel?
- Name your favorite pink thing in this book. Why is it your favorite?
- Name your favorite pink thing at home. Why is it your favorite?
- Can you tell how the people in the picture feel by looking at their faces?
  Do you ever feel the same way? When? Why?

TRY SOMETHING NEW... Brighten someone's day! Share some strawberry ice cream or your favorite snack with a friend!

community of color series

8000 210 770186